In These Houses

Also by Brenda Marie Osbey
Ceremony for Minneconjoux
Desperate Circumstance, Dangerous Woman

In These Houses

Brenda Marie Osbey

Wesleyan University Press
Middletown, Connecticut

Some of the poems in this book appeared originally in *The American Poetry Review*, *The American Voice*, *Callaloo*, *The Greenfield Review*, *The Southern Review*, and *Woman Poet: The South*. "Portrait" received an AWP Poetry Competition Award and was published in *Tendril*.

The excerpt from "The Love Song of J. Alfred Prufrock" from *Collected Poems* by T. S. Eliot, copyright © 1936 by T. S. Eliot, is reprinted by permission of Harcourt Brace Jovanovich, Inc. and Faber and Faber Ltd. The excerpt from "O Daedalus Fly Away Home" from *Selected Poems* by Robert Hayden, copyright © 1966 by Robert Hayden, is reprinted by permission of October Press Inc.

To the following, my deepest gratitude for the invaluable professional and personal support extended to me, and a constant and demonstrated faith in my work: Chris Barnes and The MacDowell Colony, Ann Bookman, Elizabeth McKinsey and The Mary Ingraham Bunting Institute, Victor Perera and Charles H. Rowell.

All inquiries and permissions requests should be addressed to the Publisher, Wesleyan University Press, 110 Mt. Vernon Street, Middletown, Connecticut 06457.

This book is supported by a grant from the National Endowment for the Arts.

Library of Congress Cataloging-in-Publication Data

Osbey, Brenda Marie.
   In these houses/Brenda Marie Osbey.—1st ed.
     p.   cm.—ᵛ(Wesleyan poetry)
   ISBN 0-8195-2146-9 ISBN 0-8195-1147-1 (pbk.)
   I. Title.   II. Series.
PS3565.S3315   1987
811'.54—dc19   87-33297
                                 CIP

Manufactured in the United States of America

FIRST EDITION

WESLEYAN POETRY

This book is dedicated to
Lois Emelda Hamilton, my mother,
in whose house my bones were cast
and called by name.

Contents

1 HOUSES OF THE SWIFT EASY WOMEN

*a man could get lost
in such a house as this*

"In These Houses of Swift Easy Women"

In the room the women come and go
Talking of Michelangelo.
　　　　　　—T. S. Eliot, "The Love Song of J. Alfred Prufrock"

in these houses
of swift easy women
drapes and the thin panels between them
hug to the walls—
some promise of remembering,
litanies of minor
pleasures and comforts.

these women know subtlety
sleight of hand
cane liquor
island songs
the poetry of soundlessness

a man could get lost
in such a house as this
could lose his way
his grasp of the world
between the front room
and the crepe myrtle trees out back.

Thelma

Oh Thelma! Thelma! with your jumping jack . . .
—from a popular song, 1920s

they say that thelma was so loose
she couldn't even hold onto herself
spent life so fast
would have to go back to old lovers
to sound out her name.
and how could we know what went on
in that house down on onzaga street?
we saw her every day.
she'd make the young ones work
and the old ones work hard.
and we could see them all dancing
and calling *jesus jesus* in the broad daylight.
and now
not a one of them can tell you
what it was she did to them
or made them do.
one of them told
how thelma came unstopped one day
and nothing could hold her after that
and after that
she never held onto nothing.
it finally caught up with thelma, he said.
i saw her heading out the front door
naked as she come into the world
and before i could say a word
thelma was out in the middle of the neutral ground
dancing and screaming
eating the black dirt
calling freedom
freedom.

Beauty

ophelia's house is surrounded by growing things
she picks whatever grows
sets all kinds of flowers
about her bedroom
i must have beautiful things, she says
always about me.
i remember jonathan
never did want me to have no flowers.
never did know what it meant to me
to have a little beauty.
when i was in infirmary
they never would let me have no beauty.

ophelia smiles
dresses her hair
in mourning braids.

now halbert was different.
they all are you know.
but halbert worked in all kind of weather
and in the evening
he'd bring me peaches in honey.
i'd suck the parsley off the top
and throw it out the side-door.
halbert would just smile at me.
he was sweet-natured like that.
he gave me these feathers for my hair
and that palmetto fan on the wall.

ricard. ricard was just for pleasure
nothing but pleasure.
he thought i was a young fool.
after ricard was berthaw.

i remember the day i told him
"berthaw?
you don't mean me a bit of good
you
and none like you."

infirmary?
infirmary wasn't so bad.
neither is mississippi river water.
but i don't see you beating the band to get yours.
and the flowers?
that's for my beauty.
i keep me some beauty here in my bedroom
and keep my lovers
long dead.

Clarissa

Evil woman, evil woman / can't you see where you're falling?
oh evil woman / the devil is calling.
                    —from the blues, "Evil Woman"

she was standing on the little foot-bridge
when the man they called diamond called out
reva, he says
reva, i don't want no truck with you
no truck at all
you said you was leaving
you sure did say it
how come you had to go that way?

he was pleading.
he had ugly yellow flecks
in one grey eye.
she stood there
watching him ring his hand around
in the naked air
asking her why she wouldn't come home.
and when she thought she'd had enough
she began to walk
slowly enough for him to follow
pointing his fingers
all of them
at her slender back
calling out to people watching
she won't come home
she won't come home no more
make her somebody
make her do right to me
they turned their eyes
only their eyes.
come back reva
don't make me be no fool

at the door to the house
she is afraid to go in.
ms turner the landlady
will not know what to make of it.
and she'll be sober today
or at least not drunk.
but from the side of her eye now
she can see
the man they call diamond
is crawling in the hot dust.
i'm sorry
she turns to him.
i'm sorry
she says to him.
but my name is clarissa.
did you hear me mister?
not reva
clarissa.

the next morning
adelaide turner found the man diamond
hanging from her front porch
letters clotted in blood
on his grey-colored forehead
reva reva it said.
we found clarissa standing barefoot
in the side-alley
and we could not make her
look away.
days later
she was still mumbling
about the ugly yellow flecks
in that man's
one grey eye.

Letter Home

Darling Henry,
This is my last letter home.
Did you get Louise to take care of the children?
I do not miss them.
I miss my house.
And I miss my backyard.
People are crazy here.
I am lucky Father Dorelle was on my side.
And I ought to tell you, Henry
I lied to get his help.
Told him I had lost my faith
but then I had this vision of glory.
Now he comes every day
to see how the new-found soul is faring.
He will come Wednesday when I am released.
Father Dorelle says if I had prayed first
I never would be here now.
But then,
if Darling Henry had not driven me
till I saw fit to run stark naked
out into the neutral ground screaming freedom
I would not be here now.
Father Dorelle says I must pray
and confess my faith daily.
And I do pray now, Henry.
I pray to God you are not in my house
when I get loose from here Wednesday
because I have *most absolute faith*
that while I might not can be free of you,
Lord knows I can kill you.
And I can see to it you stay dead
on a daily basis.
Your loving woman,
Thelma V. Picou

Little Eugenia's Lover

and little eugenia
with her hispanic lover
an awkward pipe in his hand
wanting not to seem *ethnic*
wanting not to look
as though he knew the calinda
remembered the pristine clarity
of streams cutting through lost cities
preferring to seem
european
and slightly out of step
as though he could forget he had read
garcía lorca's
black and green lines.

eugenia could not know what she represents
diamond trove
deep in the amazon river
lost worlds he owned
before his color faded out.
and diving down again and again
he loses her
between a smooth coffee skin
and the jaded walls
of a city he sees quite clearly
but can not name.

eugenia talks of pleasure
of family and food
books she reads
and places on the mantlepiece
her girlhood
in an ordinary brown family.
he watches her talk

raw diamond in her eyes
mango where her mouth should be
showers her with gifts
clothes and furs
stockings and hats
anything that will cover her
anything to fade out
the walls of his lost nameless city

until she can no longer bear it
the words he says
the plundering of her body
even in her sleep
searching out lost mines he calls it
hands and lips rummaging
foundering
until she lies beneath him one morning
some heavy object in his hand
her head hanging off the bed

even in jackson he continues to insist:

there is no blood on my hands
only diamonds and mortar
that ran down from her mouth.

The Wastrel-Woman Poem

she goes out in the night again
wastreling about
her thin-woman blues
slung over one shoulder
an empty satchel
one carries out of habit.

the first time you see her
you think her body
opens some new forbidden zone.
you think she has something to do with you.
she never does.
at least not the way you mean.
not here
not any more.
lives ago perhaps
she would have been
your second cousin
a lover who murdered you
a woman who passed you on market-day
threw bones to the ground
or stepped over you
as though you were dust or air
some spirit she knew of
but did not counsel.

the first time you see her
a story begins
that has nothing to do with you:
a woman uncle feather knew
and never told you of.
you were so young
and one day he lost the connection
between your question
and her name.

her name could have been anything
but you never would know.
she would pass
and look into your eyes
directly
as if you were not there
as if she knew it
and would not tell.

tak-o-mè-la
tak-o-mè-la

something you hear when she passes
sounds from another living
but there she is
wastreling about you.

someone calls to you.
you watch your thin-woman move
between baskets of fish
and date-wine bottles.

you turn to answer

heart like a brick
down between your knees.

2 HOUSE OF MERCIES

making her exit
from this house of mercies

The Bone-Step Women

i do not hear the words
the women speak on touro street
i only see them moving
in vertical lines
their hands angled out
from their hips and thighs

i know they are singing
but i do not know the song.

they separate my bones
into neat white stacks
moving them in the dust
like bits of stone
one finds something of interest
in the way they are cast
ramshackle
on the side of the road
stirs them into dustclouds
sends up a slipshod rain
her own aging joints
toil toward motion

she is dancing in the dust
between the alleys of my bones.

House of Mercies

the structure is wood
painted white
a defiance of sorts.
but what you will notice
is the women
who enter late in the evening
and leave before daybreak.
what is it they hold
close to their skirts
so as not to have it taken
suddenly away?
you will notice how different they seem
coming and going
collapsible women
entering a wood-framed house
fully clothed
going quickly
even running
up the front walk
so careful when they leave
to close the rusted page-fence gate
looking about
some cherished article
almost covered in the folds of their skirts
bare feet slapping the paved sidewalk:

no woman swaggers or smiles
making her exit
from this house of mercies.

Sister and the Shadowman

oh sister
something about the shadowman
coming in the evening
telling about the dark
and the things we do there
oh sister!
bound by blindstitches
needles of dust
tacking us together
satins and lace
fountain pens and parchment
fried okra and fresh shrimp
oh sister
shadowman telling secrets
we don't even need to hear

blindstitch
to blindstitch
to blood.

Elvena

1.
there is a house down on old roman street
all the women pass through.
one stands outside the gate
bare feet
broad skirts gathered loosely
about her hips.
have you lost anything today?
tell me, neighbor
what have you lost today?
and her madness is a conju
slung like rope about the heart.
i said i feel her madness like a conju
like a rope
slung round my heart.

do you see elvena?
she got that way touching neighbor-women
on the edges of their fingers.
do you see that bone-step walk she walks?
and the women who go by
looking past her face
past the ash-black hands
pretending they do not see her
and nothing has been lost?
a woman can go so far out
there never will be a way back.
and there are things a woman will do
can't be learned
and won't be understood.
but somebody's got to be a witness.
don't tell me you don't see that woman
moving barefoot along the bankette.

2.
a woman goes barefoot along the bankette this evening.
no one speaks her name.
the neighbor-people have difficulty recalling her—
and no one ever remembers a woman
as she once was.

there is a neighbor-woman out there
a long ways from shoring
throw out your shimmy straps
and roll that woman in

who will touch her now?
who?
the mothers with their prayer-bands
wound tight about their wrists and waists?
the widows stabbing bricked pavements
with their low-heeled shoes,
little beads of sweat just visible above the lips,
the pearls of mourning strung effortless across their bosoms?
maybe the younger sisters she taught so well,
the school-girls who skip and prance with ease?
or else the ones riding by
on hips a man would shout over?
a neighbor-woman stands outside the gate this evening.
somebody's got to be a witness
somebody ought to call her name

3.
i used to be a woman other people called by name.
lived in a house
where the blues clung to the ceilings
to all the doors and the side-porch
and all around my garden
out back of the house.

i used to go out to that garden
and sing all the blues i could find.
you'd be surprised how much blues can grow
between the hidden-lily and the monkey-grass
overnight.

the man next door
was from somewhere out in the country.
was making a kind of cloth
worked at it all the time.
i would see him standing back in the shadows.
i could tell he was listening
and sometimes i thought he said my name—
as if it meant something.
he never did.
just stood there in the shadows
working that cloth
and listening to my blues.
sometimes i wondered
what kind of blues
that man had learned to make or give.
and sometimes i wondered
if he put my song into that cloth
and what he might have lost besides.

and tell me, neighbor
what have you lost today?

4.
only the bone-step women
would ever come for her in broad daylight
carrying their satchels of longing
like easy parcels on turbaned heads.
carrying that woman along
between the folds of their red cotton skirts
calling aloud, to no one in particular

tell the truth
tell the truth and do right
carrying that woman along like one more burden
one more parcel
that amounts to nothing much
moving along the broken road
that leads to bayou st. john.

elvena could walk among them
bare feet keeping time
to the bones up on their heads.
tell the truth, i could hear them shout.
tell the truth and do right
i know you are a witness
just tell the truth and do right

5.
the bone-step women do not come.
i sit on my front-porch into the night.
i am working colored cloth
from cuts of used string.
i see elvena when she steps down from the bankette.
i see her step
into the empty street
ash-black hands turned out
palms facing toward me.
i hold up the unfinished cloth-piece
and she begins to sing:

tell me, neighbor
what that blues is made from
tell me
tell me
i want to know
what have you lost today?

How I Became the Blues

1.
it was
dancing in mid-air
with an old half-crazed
smooth-skinned gentleman
his knees moving
at an angular plane
that i became the blues
against an afternoon glazed in mint
or van-van.
it was this urge of his
to only keep moving
as long as there was daylight
as long as there was darkness
the length of arms and legs
their own shadows
circling them
at a slower ragged pace.
and all he asked
was that i move with him
like so
he kept saying
like so
like breathing
or waiting for someone to lean at you
like a too-hungry lover
hesitating
and so he bruised me with this blues
his lips at a distance
from the hairs on my left ear.

2.
come and dance
with an old man
honey.

i'm tired of learning to do it
with my hand glued to the air.
there is nothing past this body for me
nothing past this white cotton shirt.
lean on me a little bit
where the hurt used to be.

that was how he called it:
where the hurt used to be.

3.
i call it dancing
because i have no other name for it
this old man
dreaming onto my forehead
moving me
urging me
past this blues
past endurance
to where i can not hold up my body
much less be required to dance
to keep sane the connection
between a starched white shirt
and an aged body.
and so i am leaning on his past
my feet and the rest of me
going on inside him
until the two of us realize
there is no name for this.
and even though we sing
the only words in town tell us:

it was like this
it was like so
just so
where the hurt used to be.

The House

i can not hear myself
over the hum of small-town heat
and i am not getting
the sound i need:

"we had to pay
to have the ice-man deliver then.
the girls would refuse food;
they liked to lick the ice so much."

in this place
people create fictions around foreigners
and 1954 cadillacs.
where i come from
there are stories to houses like this.
you go inside for the first time
it is stories come out to meet you:

"it was years before we could afford gas.
we cooked in the fireplace.
there was a bloodstain right out front of it.
folks round d'abadie street
said she killed him,
said she put that meat cleaver in him
and cut out his heart.
the girls never fought too bad in that house.

they'd stand on the stairlanding
looking down at the fire.
you could hear their child-talk:
        'say she cut it right out.'

        'fed it to her cat.'

        '. . . and watched him eat it.'

they do say she stayed in there with that body,
waiting for her people to come.
that stain will never move."

2.

"i have never been one for carrying tales.
he-say-she-say would easy get you killed
in assumption parish.
but to tell the truth,
that augustine bears watching.
a child like that will bring turmoil."

"or sorrow,
for sure."

3.

loving this house
a neighbor-woman stands on the porch.
the weight of her words
bears into my gut:

"you'll have no peace in this house, neighbor.
you are like those women people read about:
the kind who cut and scream."

4.
more than a week it went on.
the sound drove her sisters crazy.
augustine's mother went into her room:
it was a mourning dove.
on the ninth night, augustine quite willingly
set it free.

when her sisters tired of it
the neighbor-women took it up.
    "nature"
    "nature"
she heard them say
from behind the false safety
of their close-knit porches.

augustine wore a smile bore no one malice.
her mother said she was just
peculiar.

    "like that noise;
    where'd it come from?
    her mama says to me it was a pet,
    a bird."

    "i tell you that girl ain't right."

    "my boy skite,
    he stopped her the other evening,
    asked her where she was going
    riding that de saix bus.
    that girl never did say a word.
    and you know for a fact
    everybody round here knows my skite."

    "well.
    and no good ever come of jumonville.
    i can tell you for sure.
    but that's where i seen her myself.
    i used to go there to get read my own self.
    that's where i got read about my rodney
    and that milner tramp.
    no good come of that,
    did it?"

5.

    "child, i can't help you.
    but i can feel with my hands
    and i believe you have a gift.
    i can teach you what i know.
    you can do what i do
    you can out-do me.
    ask your mama
    to let you learn."

augustine shone in things
there was no need to shine in.
her sisters took up their tales.
they went to their mother;
it did no good.
    "let her be," she said
    "for jesus' sake
    just let her be."

6.

    "it was a monday morning.
    we come downstairs
    and found augustine scrubbing the stain.
    she had the big scrub brush
    suds everywhere,
    working at that bloodstain.
    she worked long after breakfast.
    no one thought to stop her.
    and late that evening
    she went on to see doc, like always.
    no one knows what he told her.
    but when she come in
    we were putting on dinner.
    augustine went to the upstairs bathroom
    and then she come down
    and lit a fire in the fireplace.

nobody knows what he told her.

augustine stood in plain view of the kitchen.
she ate rat poison
and threw the box in the fire."

3 HOUSE OF BONES

building the structure
the years have torn down

Fly Away Home

weaving a wish and a weariness together
  to make two wings
  O fly away home fly away
      —Robert Hayden, "O Daedalus Fly Away Home"

before my first morning coffee
often i sit and weave
my wishes
my wearinesses
into one
planning my escape

hand-woven wings
lift over telephone wires

amid all the laughter
i manage to fly away home
have yet to perish
in the sea.

Consuela

What can you do
Consuela Consuela?
What can you do?
Consuela is you!

We can do it too
Consuela Consuela! . . .
    —from "Consuela! Consuela!" a girls' ring game
    played in New Orleans, ca. 1935–1965

what can you do
consuela
consuela
what can you do
consuela is you

she pays them no mind.
she knows the sounds
are not meant for her.
it's a game.
her mother played it
when she was a girl.

the prayer-women
in cotton print dresses
break the children's circle
only barely noticing
the shaking bodies
no breasts
no behinds.
consuela sees them shatter the ring.
they are omens of something

death
most likely.

in consuela's head
they are laid out in coffins
silver lamé
elbow-length gloves.

consuela makes the sign of the cross
turns her back
on the children's broken ring.

the woman next door
rosalie st. cyr
calls the children in
gives them things to mend their laughter
fruit breads and jelly cakes.
they break off her roses
and braid them into their hair.
rosalie dresses them up
in feather hats and lace scarves.
they dance in her front parlor
with the doors wide open:

we can do it too
consuela consuela

it does no harm
it is only the old neighbor-men
don't like it.
it truly does no harm.

in the hall mirror
consuela sees herself an old woman
surrounded by young girls.
consuela is dancing
dancing in perfect rhythm
dancing to her shadow:

what can you do
consuela consuela

dancing faster and faster
around and around
consuela hears the prayer-women
off in the distance
making their second round for the day
jingling
jingling
off in the distance,
tambourines against cotton cloth
the soft stamp on broken pavement

oh choose your partner
consuela consuela

but consuela is clever.
most nights she sits rocking
in an old porch chair that is not a rocker.
consuela has learned
to dance with no partner
to sing without shattering

if you give them your song
she says
you pass on your soul

in her soul
consuela forms the ring
that will not break:

and i can do it too
consuela
consuela
i can do it too
consuela
i'm you.

The Old Women on Burgundy Street

the old women on burgundy street
braid the years
into their grey-brown-white hair.
they put patient time
into the pinning of a plait
braiding in equal
ones and twos.

for various reasons
some will braid by morning
or late evening
after supper songs
after dishes and cats
have been put away.
only once or twice
have i seen one braiding at noon.

the old women on burgundy street
drink bourbon from coffee cups
while the sun goes down.
it cures rheumatism
gout
and ailments left over
from the change-of-life.

they braid in french braids
a neat basket weave
that does not interfere
with a profile
or a bowed-down head.

some of them i have seen
braiding songs into their hair
sipping from those coffee cups
sitting out on front porches
or just inside
an open sidelight.
they do not moan
their songs have an air
of learned resignation.

Portrait

1.
i sit for my portrait on the veranda.
this was once a family house.
the landlady describes
how it must have looked:
double parlors
and of course,
this veranda.

almost without malice
i say,
we call them galleries

she looks out onto the avenue
horses in her flat blue eyes
skin like unleavened bread
brittle
and without variation.

2.
i sit for my portrait on the veranda.
the photographer pushes his lips together
explaining how tiring this will be
how he wants this perfect
does not want me
to look too dark.

3.
his name is lejamn
a burly big-waisted man
sooty colored

he takes two yellow-stained
gunmetal fingers
pushes my forehead back
tells me not to look so stern.

4.
big burly gunmetal black lejamn
fourth generation photographer
how did his grandfather make a living then?
taking pictures of smooth-skinned nieces
of lady friends from paillet-land?
too proud perhaps
to work in the city
selling dry goods to the white folk
or vegetables to the black?
no rag-man
tin-man
old-gold-and-diamond-man
these so many lives later
to push young writer women on the forehead
and tell them not to look so black.

5.
jamaica
he says for no reason
you look just like jamaica

in my head i make a dance in jamaica

he says it again

just like jamaica to me

what can i say?
i am only the material he works in
given over entirely
to technique.

6.
when i come there was no street sign
only dirt roads
dirt roads and a vegetable man
give me a ride,
a soft alligator pear,
and taken me home to his aunt sue lee.

they sent me to school in the city
him selling vegetables on the weekday
all the time taking pictures
sue lee taking in shirts from uptown whites
talking at them through me:

tell them i said
tell them i will

taking in shirts from the whites
and teaching little colored girls
to speak bon français

no one stopping to question
a little tan woman
with hollow cinnamon eyes

would white children die if they looked at her?
they looked past her narrow waist instead
mouthing instructions
saying
miz suzy
too ill-bred to know
they were taking nothing from her.

sue lee sitting on the gallery of an afternoon
talking at them through me
in english when she wanted to
to show she could pronounce
the flat dead words

waving them out of sight
the screen door standing open
them running down the front walk
and sue lee never rising
until they were past her field of vision.

i stood counting out the pieces
or the money when they had come to pay
counting the silver once
twice
slowly enough to please sue lee.

7.
i sit for my portrait on the veranda.
i, named evangeline eva marie
christened by sue lee st. clementh
and her nephew august anthony peter le jamn.

i sit completely still
on the three-quarter gallery
of the house where i was raised
by a sand-faced vegetable-man photographer
and his bon français aunt

i stare in the face of the lies i have heard.
i stare into the camera's far-sighted eye.
he asks me only once:

what is your name?

evangeline, i say
evangeline eva marie clementh

he wipes a white handkerchief across his mouth.
only the camera gives its click
and again:
click.

The Godchild

i sift soil through these fingers
rotate columbine and clumps of grass
gather misbelieve tree leaves
in a crawfish bucket
near the back steps.
out where my garden grows
i kneel in the grass
my hands to the earth
waiting to hear the sound
of burdens being lifted
and moved to the side.

indoors i press damp cloth to my face
and hear the blues
coming up from the floorboards
beneath my feet
moving up from veins of oak
and pine
calling not me
but my girlhood
spent watching and hearing
too far beyond the surface
of a woman who favored me.

olevia de congé had accustomed herself
to moving about with dust on her feet
walking through the alley
leading to her aunt lavinia's back door
she had come to associate it
with pinning up her hair
the smell of coffee.
and between that side-alley and that door
olevia was a name called out
for a niece or a godchild

to come
fetching a kerchief
or a sheet of writing paper

and putting together piecemeal
such few rags of time
as allow for movement on fresh soil
olevia would lay back a collar
place a bracelet just so
and move past the palm trees out back.

i could only tell she was bending
hands cupped
and held way out front.
it wasn't until she was on her knees
it wasn't until she looked up
and saw me watching,
the water rolling down her forehead,
that she knew i was her godchild.

years later
i heard her sing for the first time
her voice coming up
from miss lavinia's bedcovers.
she called me to that bedroom
to hear her sing
and i ran
from the sound of the screen door banging
to that bed where she refused to struggle.
the sound in her throat
too much sound for a dying woman to be making
too much sound for the living
for the young
for the watching.

in that death-bed
i found embroidered kerchieves
and half-written letters
and so many objects
i have never learned the names of.
i planted them all out back
at the foot of the misbelieve tree.
i pressed the soil with my bare foot.
i pressed my godmother's life
with one bare foot.

Geography

the geography i am learning
has me place myself
at simultaneous points
of celebration
and all you see and hear in me
is these women
walking in the middle of the road
with their hoodoo in their hands.

this map leads you to a desert-place
and flowers daring brilliance
in the most cruel and merciless sun
and all you see for miles around
these women
tender past hurting
visibly bruised
only on the very edges.

this place no one chooses
is the land i tarry in.
this ritual i go through
is as old as its name
and the prophet-women who dance it:

first you place one foot
and then the other

this map has been used before.
you have seen these travelers
all their hoodoo
walking behind them
in the dust:

first you place one foot

this journey has been made before
in the middle of the day
your friends and your family
carrying this same hoodoo
leaving you behind:

first you place one foot
and then the other

i said
first you place *one* foot.

this body has done
its share of the journey.

House of Bones

you move backwards.
your heels finding the land
they have traveled before
leading in the other
safer direction.
do not trust these feet
to get you there.
they have lied to you before
and this would not be the first time
they had taken you by a road
that shows you nothing you will need
to make this journey.
do not let them take you
by any other way.

once you find the place
this is what you must do:
begin building
your hands behind your back
begin building
from scraps of living
lying idle and thirsty
begin building
from almost nothing
working in the dark
your face in the other direction.
never look back on your work
building the structure
the years have torn down.

and as you work
without proper materials
or light of day
these are the words you must recite.
repeat them daily
until you hear how true they are:

this is the house
i have carried inside me
this is the house
made of artifact and gut
this is the house
all my bones have come from
this is the house
nothing
nothing
nothing can tear down.

Glossary of Louisiana Ethnic Expressions and Place Names

alligator pear   avocado

Assumption Parish   one of sixty-four Louisiana parishes (counties elsewhere)

bankette   paved or boarded sidewalk

doc   doctor; in New Orleans Hoodoo and Spiritualist tradition, one who employs roots, herbs, and ritual to heal body and mind, thus often referred to as a "two-headed doctor"

gallery   Louisiana designation for the circular or semicircular porch common to large houses; pronounced "gal'ry"

Jackson   the Louisiana state mental institution

misbelieve tree   New Orleans designation for the Japanese plum tree common to the area; a mild table wine is made from the bright orange fruit

mothers   common designation for women who serve as healers, especially those affiliated with the formal Spiritualist Church or who operate private chapels

nature   reference to the sexual energy of an individual, said by Hoodoos and Spiritualists to be capable of endowing characteristics of greatness or madness in individuals depending on how it is channeled; said especially of women

Paillet-land   tract of land, in what is now New Orleans' Seventh Ward (one of seventeen municipal districts), formerly a plantation owned by Creole slaveholder Paillet and later the center of black "Creoleville"; pronounced "pàh-lay"

sidelight   one of two narrow doors on either side of the main door to a house; common architectural feature in New Orleans and, during warm-weather months, left open for added ventilation and easy access to the outdoors; typically used to observe the activities of neighbors and passers-by

to be read   to obtain spiritual interpretation of one's
life, present and future difficulties, or health
matters through intercession and services of
a Spiritualist; consequently, to be advised
on how to counteract undesirable develop-
ments in one's affairs through performance
of the prescribed rituals

van-van   Creole for vervain; herb used to conjure and
to heal; sometimes said to promote
affection and fond memories

About the Author

Brenda Marie Osbey is a native of New Orleans. She received a B.A. from Dillard University (1978), attended the Université Paul Valéry at Montpéllier, France, and received an M.A. from the University of Kentucky (1986). She has taught French and English at Dillard University and was curator for the Louisiana division of the New Orleans Public Library. Osbey won the Academy of American Poets 1980 Loring-Williams Prize and a 1984 AWP (Associated Writing Programs) Award. She has been a fellow of the Fine Arts Work Center at Provincetown, the Kentucky Foundation for Women, the MacDowell Colony, the Millay Colony, and the Bunting Institute of Radcliffe College, Harvard University. She is the author also of *Ceremony for Minneconjoux* and *Desperate Circumstance, Dangerous Woman,* a work-in-progress. She lives in New Orleans.

About the Book

In These Houses was composed on the Mergenthaler 202 in Galliard, a contemporary rendering of a classic typeface prepared for Mergenthaler in 1978 by the British type designer Matthew Carter. The book was composed by G&S Typesetters of Austin, Texas, and designed and produced by Kachergis Book Design, Pittsboro, North Carolina.